LIONS:
Kings of the Jungle
(Wildlife Big Cats)

SPEEDY
PUBLISHING

Speedy Publishing LLC

40 E. Main St. #1156

Newark, DE 19711

www.speedypublishing.com

The lion is a member of the Cat family and one of the five big cats.

Lions are the second largest big cat species in the world second only to the tiger. The average male lion weighs around 180 kg while the average female lion weighs around 130 kg.

Lions live in grasslands, scrub, and open woodlands of sub-Saharan Africa. Lions in the wild live for around 12 years.

Lions are very social animals. They live in groups that are called prides. Prides can be as small as 3 or as big as 40 animals.

Lions are carnivores, which means they live on meat. Their prey consists mainly of large mammals such as wildebeest, impalas, zebras, buffalo, and warthogs.

Male lions are easy to recognize because of their distinctive manes. Males with darker manes are more likely to attract lionesses.

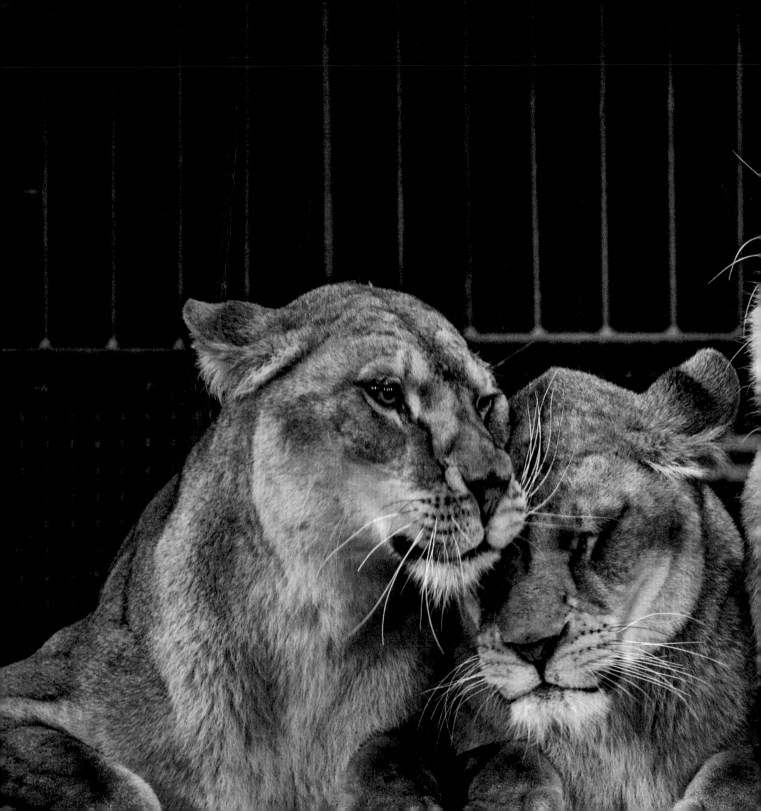

Lions are the laziest of the big cats. They usually spend 20 hours a day sleeping and resting.

White lions are the same as any other lion, but with white fur. The white lion is a rare color mutation.

Made in the USA
Lexington, KY
14 November 2017